Romans, Saxons & Vikings

Living in Viking Britain

Martyn Whittock

KU-243-447

30158133

941·01/Whi

First published in Great Britain by
Heinemann Library
Halley Court, Jordan Hill, Oxford OX2 8EJ
a division of Reed Educational & Professional
Publishing Ltd

MELBOURNE AUCKLAND
FLORENCE PRAGUE MADRID ATHENS
SINGAPORE TOKYO CHICAGO SAO PAULO
PORTSMOUTH NH MEXICO
IBADAN GABORONE JOHANNESBURG
KAMPALA NAIROBI

© Reed Educational & Professional
Publishing Ltd 1996

All rights reserved. No part of this publication may
be reproduced, stored in a retrieval system, or
transmitted in any form or by any means,
electronic, mechanical, photocopying, recording,
or otherwise without either the prior written
permission of the Publishers or a licence permitting
restricted copying in the United Kingdom issued by
the Copyright Licensing Agency Ltd, 90 Tottenham
Court Road, London W1P 9HE

Designed by Ken Vail Graphic Design

Origination by Magnet Harlequin Group

Illustrations by Ken Vail Graphic Design

Printed in the UK by Jarrold Book Printing, Thetford

00 99 98 97 96

10 9 8 7 6 5 4 3 2 1

ISBN 0 431 05968 3

British Library Cataloguing in Publication Data

Whittock, Martyn J. (Martyn John)
Living in Viking Britain. – (Romans, Saxons,
Vikings)
1. Great Britain – History – Anglo-Saxon period,
449 – 1066 – Juvenile literature
2. Great Britain – Social life and customs – To 1066
– Juvenile literature
I. Title II. Series 941'.016

Every effort has been made to contact copyright
holders of any material reproduced in this book.
Any omissions will be rectified in subsequent
printings if notice is given to the Publisher.

Acknowledgements

The Publishers would like to thank
the following for permission to
reproduce photographs. Ancient Art
and Architecture Collection: p.13;
British Museum: p.4, p.5, p.21, p.27;
Cambridge University Library: p.27;
CM Dixon: p.11; James Lang: p.8;
Museum of London: p.24; National
Museum of Dublin: p.17p; Ordnance
Survey: p.7; Ray Sutcliffe: p.19;
Statens Historiska Museum: p.29;
Universitetets Oldsaksamling: p.23;
York Archaeological Trust: p.15

Cover photograph reproduced with
permission of The British Museum.

Our thanks to Keith Stringer, of the
Department of History of Lancaster
University, for his comments in the
preparation of this book.

We would like to thank the following
schools for valuable comments made
regarding the content and layout of
this series: Fitzmaurice Primary
School, Bradford-on-Avon, Wiltshire;
Tyersal School, Bradford, Yorkshire.
Thanks also to Linda James, Jorvik
Viking Centre, York.

Details of written sources

C. Fell, *Women in Anglo-Saxon
England*, British Museum
Publications 1984: 13A

G. Garmonsway, *Anglo-Saxon
Chronicle*, Dent 1972: 1A; 4A

M. Gibson, *The Vikings*,
Wayland 1972: 12B

M. Magnusson, *Vikings*,
BCA 1980: 1D; 6B

J. Nichol, *The Vikings*,
Blackwell 1979: 11A

**For Emma Bailey, with love
from Uncle Martyn.**

Contents

Clues from the past

The Vikings first attacked Britain in AD789. They later settled in many parts of Britain.

In AD1013, a Viking, Swein Forkbeard, became king of England. This Viking control of England lasted until 1042. Different kinds of clues survive from this time. These clues can tell us about life in Viking Britain.

The Vikings had different ideas about art to the **Anglo-Saxons**. They put this art on **brooches** and carvings. Vikings spoke different languages to the Anglo-Saxons and made up new place-names.

The Anglo-Saxons wrote about the Vikings, who had invaded their country. But we have to be careful about how we use many of these clues. Also, many people could not read or write. So we know more about the things people made, like pots or houses, than about what they thought or felt.

Source A

Terrible warnings appeared in Northumbria. There were great flashes of lightning. Fiery dragons were seen in the air. That same year the enemies of God horribly destroyed God's church in Lindisfarne.

From the Anglo-Saxon Chronicle, AD793.
It tells how the Vikings attacked Britain. But can we trust it? Anglo-Saxons hated Vikings and wanted them to sound bad – and the part about the dragons sounds unreal.

Source B

A Viking sock from York. It is made from wool. This survived because the ground was wet. If it had been dry it would have rotted away. Lots of clues about the Vikings have been lost.

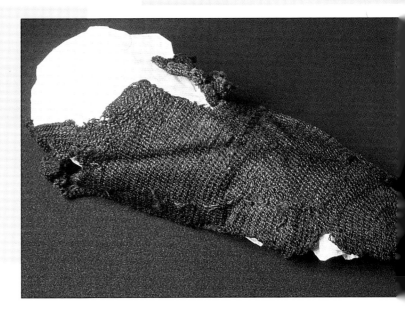

4

Source C

Looking down on the site of a Viking farm, on the Isle of Man. Many Vikings seem to have lived in the same kinds of houses as Anglo-Saxons. Often we cannot tell from the site who were Anglo-Saxons and who were Vikings.

Source D

I praise the king throughout his land. And keenly sing his open hand.

Vikings wrote stories called **sagas**. *But we do not know if we can trust them. This is 'Egil's Saga', about a Viking* **king** *of York. It was written in about AD1220. This was a long time after the events in the story.*

Most sagas were written long after the people in the stories really lived. Most were written in countries other than Britain.

Source E

A Viking brooch from Goldsborough, in Yorkshire. It is decorated with the art that Vikings liked. But other people might have copied Viking art. Some of the people with Viking brooches might really have been Anglo-Saxons.

Where did the Vikings live?

The Vikings raided Britain at first, then settled here later.

The Vikings came from what are now the countries of Denmark and Norway. From about AD789, they began pirate raids on Britain. From about AD874, Vikings began to settle in Britain. They defeated many of the Anglo-Saxon armies. They took over parts of Britain.

Source A

These are Hogback gravestones. They are a kind of carving that was popular with some Vikings. They were probably placed on the site where a Viking leader was buried.

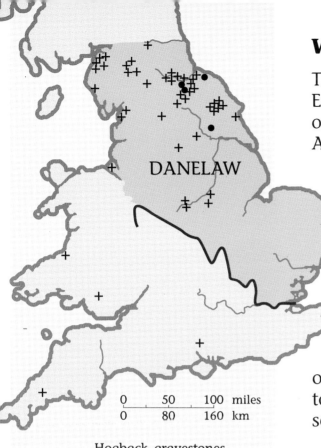

Hogback gravestones

+ One grave found

● Five or more found

▬ Edge of the Danelaw

Map to show where Hogback gravestones are found in Britain.

Where did the Vikings settle?

The Vikings mostly settled in the north of England, in the Midlands and in the east of England. The Vikings conquered the Anglo-Saxon kings of Northumbria, East Anglia and Mercia. They took over the running of these kingdoms. This part of England became known as the **Danelaw.** This was because the Danes (Vikings) ran this area with their own laws.

The Vikings did not beat the Anglo-Saxon kings of Wessex. This kingdom was in the south and west of England. The Vikings were not able to take over this land. Other Vikings settled in Scotland, Wales and Ireland.

Clues about settlements

We can tell where Vikings settled from things like the kinds of carved stones that they liked. Some of these are called Hogback gravestones.
They are decorated in a way that was popular with Vikings.

How do we know?

Source A shows us the special kinds of carvings popular with some Vikings settlers. The map shows that these were popular in only some parts of Britain.

These clues show Vikings settled in certain parts of the country.

In other parts of Britain there are hardly any of the Hogback gravestones. Viking **lords** and **warriors** did not take over the land in these parts of Britain.

But there are parts of Viking Britain where these carvings are not found. So not all Vikings liked these special carvings.

9

Different people in the Viking countryside

Viking leaders took land from people they defeated. They gave it to their own followers.

When the Vikings came to Britain it was already full of people farming the land. Before they came, most of Britain was divided up into **estates.** These were large areas of land run by **Anglo-Saxon kings,** large churches and rich Anglo-Saxon **lords.**

Breaking up estates

The Viking leaders, or 'Jarls', were rich and powerful, fighting men. They took land from the Anglo-Saxons and gave it to their own followers. In the **Danelaw**, these followers soon owned land of their own. These small farmers were called 'karls', or 'sokemen'.

Who worked the land?

The people who worked on the land for the Vikings would have been poorer Anglo-Saxons. Some of them would have been **slaves** or 'thralls'. They did the hardest work. They were people captured in wars, or punished for crimes, or they were from the families of these people.

There would also have been priests living in the countryside, leading worship in the Christian churches. Many Vikings soon became Christians.

Source A

The Viking army went from Cirencester into East Anglia and settled there and shared out the land.

The Anglo-Saxon Chronicle, from the year AD880.

Source B

Thralls carry wood and herd animals. Karls care for oxen, make ploughs and farm. Jarls ride horses, play with dice, go swimming. They fight wars and kill doomed people.

A Viking poem. It describes the different kinds of people living in the countryside.

A carving of a wealthy Viking lord, or Jarl. It was carved on a stone cross. It comes from Middleton, in Yorkshire.

How do we know?

Source A tells us that when the Vikings captured areas of Britain they split up the land amongst themselves.

Source B shows that different kinds of people lived in the countryside. They did different types of jobs. The hardest jobs were done by slaves.

Source C shows us what a rich Viking Jarl looked like. He has a helmet, a spear, a shield and a sword. This shows that Jarls were powerful, fighting people. Also, only a rich and powerful person could have paid for a carving like this. This shows how important these Viking leaders were.

Living in the countryside – Viking farmhouses

The farmhouses where Vikings lived changed when they came to Britain.

Most Vikings lived in the countryside. Before the Vikings came to Britain they often lived in houses called longhouses. In the longhouses, people lived at one end of the house, and farm animals lived at the other end.

Viking farmhouses in Britain

In Britain, Vikings lived in large **halls.** The walls were often made from sticks woven together and covered with mud. This is called **wattle and daub.** At times, farmhouses were made from stone.

Sometimes the wooden walls had curved sides. Sometimes there was a high part at one end. The Viking **lord** might have sat here. There were often benches along the walls. Servants of the lord sat there. They slept there, too.

These were not longhouses. Animals did not live there. Viking settlers changed how they made their houses. They copied **Anglo-Saxon** halls, and lived like Anglo-Saxon lords. In north Scotland, some still used longhouses.

Source A

In those days farmsteads usually had large halls in them. The men sat by the fire in the evening. Tables were put up in front of them at mealtimes. After meals they lay down and slept near the fire. During the day women worked there weaving with wool.

A description of life in a Viking hall. It comes from a Viking story called 'Grettir's Saga'. It was written in about AD1320.

Source B

The ruins of Viking farmhouses. These had walls made of stone and earth. They are on the island of Orkney, in Scotland.

How do we know?

Source A tells us that Viking men ate and slept in the hall. It also tells us that there were benches around the side to sit on and sleep on.

Source B shows that Viking farmhouses were big. Some, in Scotland, had stone walls. But most Viking houses in Britain had wooden walls. These rot away. This makes it harder to imagine what they looked like.

Relaxing at home

The Vikings enjoyed different ways of relaxing and enjoying themselves.

Feasting and storytelling

Rich and powerful Vikings loved feasts and storytelling. At these feasts they ate and drank a lot. There were three main feasts a year. One was at the beginning of the year. Another was in April. The last was at the end of October.

After the feasts, there was often storytelling. The people who told the stories were called skalds. The skalds told many kinds of stories. Some stories were old ones they had learned. Others were new ones, which they had made up. They told these stories from memory. Only much later were these stories written down.

Sagas

The stories were often about famous **kings** and **warriors.** These stories were called sagas. Often they were written down a long time after the warriors in them had died. The sagas made fighting sound exciting.

Source A

I have never heard singing which was more horrid. It is like a growl. Like dogs howling, but more horrible.

This is how a visitor to a Viking feast described the singing. This visitor was an Arab traveller. His name was Al-Tattushi. He visited the Viking town at Hedeby, in Denmark. This account of his visit was written in AD975.

Source B

My mother told me she'd buy me a longship, a handsome oared vessel, To go sailing with Vikings, To stand at the stern and steer a fine warship.

From a story called 'Egil's Saga', written in about AD1220.

Viking pipes from the town of 'Jorvik' (York). Five holes were carefully bored in a block of wood to make the pipes.

How do we know?

Source A shows that the Vikings liked to sing. But we cannot tell if their singing was really good, or bad. This is just one person's opinion. He might have disliked it because it was different to Arab music.

Source B shows that sagas made fighting sound enjoyable.

Source C shows us that Vikings liked to listen to music. The pipes can be played to hear the kinds of musical sounds made in Viking Britain.

Singing and dancing

Vikings also enjoyed listening to music. Some of the musical instruments they made have been found. Pipes called pan-pipes have been found in York. These were made out of wood. Part of a stringed instrument was also found there. It was like a **harp.** Vikings also liked singing. They sometimes sang while they danced.

Living in Viking towns

Towns grew in size. They became more important during the Viking Age.

When the Vikings first came to Britain, there were very few towns. By AD1066 there were more than 100 towns.

Why did towns become more important?

Some towns became important because the **Anglo-Saxons** built defences around them against Viking attacks. The Vikings also built defences around the towns they captured. These towns then became places where people felt safe. Things could be made there and bought and sold.

York and the Five Boroughs

York was an important Viking town. The Vikings called it 'Jorvik'. It had once been the Anglo-Saxon town of Eoforwic. It was captured by the Vikings. A new bridge was built over the river Ouse and more **craftworkers** moved into the town. Other important Viking towns made up the Five Boroughs. They were Derby, Leicester, Lincoln, Nottingham and Stamford.

Source A

It was well built and strongly made with walls. These are now old and breaking down. It is too rich to describe. It is packed with goods brought by **merchants.** They come from many countries but most are Danes. There are lots of people there. There are 30,000, not counting children.

A description of Viking 'Jorvik' (York). It is from a book called 'The Life of St Oswald', written in about AD1000.

Source B

Remains of the wooden pavement of a Viking town. This is from Dublin Here, unlike England, Vikings set up the first towns.

How do we know?

Source A shows that Jorvik was an old town. The Vikings did not set up many new towns. They captured old ones like Jorvik. These towns then grew in size. The source shows how important Jorvik became.

Source B shows that wood and wattle pathways were sometimes built in the streets. These kept people out of the mud and filth.

Life in a Viking town

Most of the buildings were made of wood, with walls of **wattle and daub.** Some buildings had floors dug into the dirt. Their walls were made of wooden planks.

In the back yards, pits were dug into the ground. Some pits were wells. Others had rubbish dumped in them. Some were used as toilets. The streets were dirty and smelly. Inside the houses it would have been cleaner. Sand was put on the rubbish pits in the back yard. This covered them over and kept the smell down! Sometimes wooden pavements were built so that people did not have to walk in the mud.

Buying and selling in Viking Britain

The Vikings were not all warriors. Some were traders, who bought and sold things.

The first Vikings attacked **Anglo-Saxon** towns. This made it hard to buy and sell things. But in time **trade** grew again. In the areas that the Vikings captured, the fighting stopped. People felt safe to travel again. This made it easier to trade once more.

What did Viking traders sell?

Viking traders came to Britain from Denmark and Norway. They brought with them walrus ivory and amber for jewellery, fur and fish. They also brought soapstone. This is soft stone. It could be carved to make bowls. Other types of stone were brought to Britain for making knife sharpeners and **millstones**. **Pottery** and wine came from France. Silk came from the Middle East.

What did Viking traders buy?

Viking traders bought wheat, wool, wine, tin, honey, silver, cloth and **slaves** in Britain.

Source A

Thorolf had a large ship for sailing across the sea. It had been carefully built. He put dried fish, skins and furs on the ship and it went west to England.

When they arrived they found a good place to buy and sell. They loaded their ship with wheat, honey, wine and cloth. In the autumn helpful winds carried them home.

An account of a Viking trader's visit to England, from a Viking story called 'Egil's Saga', written in about AD1220.

Source B

One of the most common types of pottery traded in Viking Britain. It comes from Stamford, in Lincolnshire. It has been found at many places in eastern England.

How do we know?

Source A shows that Viking traders came to Britain to buy and sell things. It shows the kinds of things that they bought and sold. They sold fish, skins and furs. They bought wheat, honey, wine and cloth.

But Source B shows that many of the things for sale in Viking markets did not come a long way. This pottery was made in this country, but was very popular.

Where did the things sold come from?

Most things sold by Viking traders in Britain came from Britain. Some Viking traders brought things to Britain from far away. But most things for sale in a Viking market came from other parts of Britain. There were 15,000 Viking objects found at Coppergate in Jorvik (York). But only 500 came from outside Britain. This shows that trade was important but not many things were carried a long way to be sold.

Viking ships

The Vikings were skilled at building ships. They built different kinds of ships for peace and war.

Vikings were able to travel great distances to raid and trade because they had well built ships. The most famous warships were called longships. They had one large sail. They were also rowed by the **warriors.** They were fast ships. The biggest of these ships were called dragonships. These ships often had a dragon, or monster, carved on the front. These frightened their enemies.

Ships for peace

Viking traders used a ship called a 'knarr'. This was shorter and wider than a longship. It had plenty of room to store things to sell. It used a sail instead of oars.

Life on the ships

Ships carried tents. Travellers could shelter in them from the wet and cold. They carried dried fish, smoked meat and barrels of drink called ale and mead.

Source A

The **king** called his ship 'The Long Serpent'. It had benches in it for 34 rowers to sit on. It had a dragon on the front and an arched tail behind, covered with gold.

A description of a Viking warship from 'Olaf Tryggvason's Saga', written in the thirteenth century.

Source B

There were twelve ships. They were covered with black tents. Light came from the tents where the men were drinking.

A description of Viking ships in a harbour, from 'Svarfdaela Saga', written in the thirteenth century.

*A Viking ship
discovered at
Oseberg, in
Norway.*

How do we know?

The information from Source A shows that Viking longships often had dragons carved on them. But not all longships had dragons on them. Source C shows that the Oseberg ship had a carefully carved spiral shape.

This ship also shows how skilful the Vikings were at cutting and carving wood to make ships. It is long and thin. This shows why such ships were called longships. This was why the king, in Source A, called his ship 'The Long Serpent'.

Source B shows us that Vikings used tents as shelter on their ships.

Workshops and craftworkers

During the Viking Age, industries grew quicker than they had at any time since the end of Roman Britain.

Craftworkers before the Vikings came to Britain

During the time when the Romans ruled Britain, **craftworkers** made many things to buy and sell. They were well organized. They made so many cheap things that even poor people could afford to buy some pots and jewellery.

When the Romans stopped ruling Britain, this stopped. The industries making things like **pottery** came to an end.

The **Anglo-Saxons** had many craftworkers but they did not make many things that ordinary people could afford. Some of them made expensive items for **kings**, **lords** and Christian churches. Other craftworkers worked in villages making a few things for their local area.

Source A

*Rings and **brooches** made from a metal called pewter. They come from London. A brooch the same as one of these has also been found in the Viking town of Dublin. They are from the tenth century* AD.

24

Source B

Early must the blacksmith who will silver earn, start at the bellows, blowing fire in blue-black coal. Singing hammer I swing, beating hard the steel, which red-hot gleams and sparkles while greedy bellows blow.

*The work of a Viking metalworker. It comes from a Viking story called a **saga**, written in the thirteenth century.*

How do we know?

Source A shows that craftworkers produced cheap brooches which many ordinary people could afford. They used cheaper metals like pewter.

Source B shows Viking blacksmiths worked hard, for money, but we cannot tell whether this person supplied just a few people, or was in a town making things for many people.

How things made by craftworkers changed

During the Viking Age, more craftworkers came to work in towns. They tried out new ways of making things. They tried to make lots of things that looked the same and were cheap. They worked hard to earn money.

Pottery and metalwork

Potters began to make cheap pots for ordinary people to buy. At first they made the pots using their hands. Then they turned the clay on a wheel. This was quicker. Soon they were making thousands of pots a year. Many had a shiny surface, called glaze.

Craftworkers began to make cheap jewellery. Ordinary people could buy this. It was made of metals like iron, pewter or lead. It was cheaper than gold or silver.

Why did these changes happen?

The Vikings did not make all these things happen. Some of them had started before the Vikings arrived. But they seem to have brought some new ideas. The new Viking lords were quite wealthy and wanted to buy things. This encouraged craftworkers to make things. People wanted to have things decorated in the kinds of styles that the Vikings liked.

Viking art and fashions

Craftworkers working in Viking Britain made things in new styles. These were popular with the Viking settlers. They were also popular with people whom the Vikings ruled.

The Vikings brought new ideas. Some were about fashion. These ideas became popular across Britain. This started between AD850 and AD950.

New patterns on brooches

Many of these new styles appeared on Viking **brooches.** These were worn on women's dresses. The brooches were decorated with carved patterns of the thin bodies of animals. Other brooches were decorated with plants. These patterns appeared on books, too.

Clothing and hair fashions

Most clothes were brightly coloured. Vikings loved colours like red, green, blue and yellow.

Vikings had different hair fashions to **Anglo-Saxons.** These Viking haircuts soon became popular with Anglo-Saxons, as well.

Source A

Do not copy Danish [Viking] haircuts. They have their necks shaved. Their hair is long at the front, hanging over one eye. It is a shameful way to dress.

A complaint by an Anglo-Saxon. It was written in the eleventh century.

Source B

She pulled down her veil, straightened her sleeves and smoothed down her **mantle.** She wore a beautiful brooch on her breast. Her blue silk dress had a long train.

A description of a rich Viking woman. It comes from a Viking book called the 'Elder Edda', written in about AD1270.

Source C

A brooch from Pitney, in Somerset. It is decorated with Viking art. The thin bodies of monsters are mixed up together. It was probably made in about AD1030.

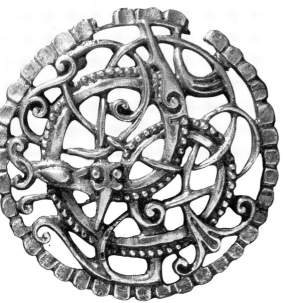

Source D

A decorated letter 'd'. It comes from a book written at Winchcombe, in Gloucestershire. It has the same kind of animal decorating it as the brooch. It was probably written in about AD1030.

How do we know?

Source A shows that Viking haircuts became popular with some Anglo-Saxons. Not everyone thought this was a good thing, though!

Source B shows the colour of a Viking woman's clothes and that she wore a brooch. But it does not tell us what the brooch was like.

Both Sources C and D show that Viking art styles were used on brooches and books. This art was popular even in areas which were not ruled by the Vikings. We know this because the brooch and book do not come from a Viking part of Britain.

Women in Viking Britain

**Women looked after life in the Viking lord's hall.
Some were rich and owned their own land.**

Women had different kinds of lives, depending on whether they were rich or poor. Rich women owned land. They were able to sell it, or give it to whoever they chose. There are a number of women with Viking names in the **Domesday Book**. They owned land in Yorkshire.

Rich, married women were expected to make sure their husband's **hall** was properly run. They often served the drinks to important guests at feasts. In Viking poems they were sometimes called 'goddesses of wine', or 'goddesses of drinking horns'.

Poorer women

Women who were poor had to work a lot harder. Some did the cooking and cleaning in the hall. Most worked on the land with their family. The hardest jobs were done by **slaves.** Women who were slaves had no choice about the jobs they did. Viking poems gave them unkind names like 'rag wearer' or 'fat legs'.

Source A

As soon as she could do anything for herself she trained more with bow and shield and sword than with needlework and embroidery.

From a Viking story about a warrior-woman. This story is called 'Hervor's Saga'. It was written in the thirteenth century.

Source B

Asa owned her land. Her husband could not control it. It was not his to give away, or sell.

From a law case about a rich Viking woman named Asa. She lived in Yorkshire in the eleventh century.

*A Viking pendant.
It comes from Sweden.
It shows a woman
carrying a drinking horn.
It comes from the tenth
century AD.*

How do we know?

Source A shows that some women fought like men. They were warriors. We cannot be sure of this, though. Most of what we know about these women comes from **sagas**. Saga writers sometimes made things up, to make an interesting story.

Source B shows that some Viking women lived independent lives. Some owned their own land. They were not controlled by their husbands.

Source C shows that women were still expected to serve guests at feasts. They carried horns filled with drink.

Divorce

Women who were not slaves were allowed to divorce their husbands. They could do this if they did not like them, or if the husband would not do what the woman wanted.

Warrior women

Some women may even have taken part in fighting. We do not know much about women like this. But there are two Irish legends about **warrior** women. At Gerdrup, in Denmark, a Viking woman was buried with a spear, like a warrior. There may have been a few women like this in Britain.

Glossary

Anglo-Saxons people living in England when the Vikings invaded

brooch jewellery used to fasten clothing together. This was important in the days before zips and buttons.

craftworkers skilled people who are able to make useful or expensive objects

Danelaw the part of England which was ruled by the Danes

Domesday Book a list of all the people who owned land when William the Conqueror ruled England. It was written in AD1086

estate a large area of land

hall the large house in which a lord lived. His family and followers lived there, too. The most powerful lords had the grandest halls. The biggest halls belonged to kings.

harp a musical instrument with strings

king the ruler of a kingdom. The Viking invaders of Britain were ruled by a number of different kings..

lords the most powerful people after a king. They were given land by the king and they would fight for him. The most powerful Viking lords were called 'Jarls'.

mantle a cloak worn by a woman

merchant a person who travels to buy and sell things

millstones heavy stones, used to grind grain into flour

pottery bowls, plates and bottles made from clay, which is heated in an oven to make it hard

settlement a group of houses, where people live together

slave someone who belongs to another person and has no freedom

trade buying and selling things

wattle and daub walls made from twigs, woven together and covered with clay, mixed with straw

warriors Vikings who fought for their lord, or king. They were rewarded with gold and silver and lived with their lord. Some warriors went on to become important lords themselves.

Timeline – Romans, Anglo-Saxons and Vikings

100BC	**AD700**
AD1	
AD100	**AD789** First Viking attacks on Britain
AD200	**AD800**
AD300	
AD400	All Anglo-Saxon kingdoms are defeated by Vikings, except for Wessex
	AD874 Vikings begin to settle in many areas of Britain. Danelaw is set up.
AD500	**AD900** Viking fashions become popular after this time
AD600	Growth in towns and trade across Britain
AD700	New Viking attacks on Britain
AD800	**AD1000**
AD900	**AD1013** Viking King Swein conquers Britain
AD1000	**AD1042** End of Viking rule in Britain

Viking Age

Index

Numbers in plain type (14) refer to the text. Numbers in italic type (*22*) refer to a caption.